Fitness Goals Tracker

Fitness Journal For Women

Activinotes

Activinotes
DAILY JOURNALS, PLANNERS, NOTEBOOKS AND OTHER BLANK BOOKS

Copyright 2016

CORE BODY	DAY 1	DAY 2	DAY 3	DAY 4	DAY 5	DAY 6
EXERCISE						
SETS						
REPS						
WEIGHTS						
REST TIME						
UPPER BODY						
EXERCISE						
SETS						
REPS						
WEIGHTS						
REST TIME						
LOWER BODY						
EXERCISE						
SETS						
REPS						
WEIGHTS						
REST TIME						

WARM UP	DAY 1	DAY 2	DAY 3	DAY 4	DAY 5	DAY 6
ACTIVITY						
SETS						
REPS						
TIME						
DIST						
INTENSITY						

COOL DOWN						
ACTIVITY						
SETS						
REPS						
TIME						
DIST						
INTENSITY						

GOALS: _____

_____

_____

_____

_____

_____

_____

_____

CORE BODY	DAY 1	DAY 2	DAY 3	DAY 4	DAY 5	DAY 6
EXERCISE						
SETS						
REPS						
WEIGHTS						
REST TIME						

UPPER BODY						
EXERCISE						
SETS						
REPS						
WEIGHTS						
REST TIME						

LOWER BODY						
EXERCISE						
SETS						
REPS						
WEIGHTS						
REST TIME						

WARM UP	DAY 1	DAY 2	DAY 3	DAY 4	DAY 5	DAY 6
ACTIVITY						
SETS						
REPS						
TIME						
DIST						
INTENSITY						

COOL DOWN						
ACTIVITY						
SETS						
REPS						
TIME						
DIST						
INTENSITY						

GOALS: _____

_____

_____

_____

_____

_____

_____

_____

CORE BODY	DAY 1	DAY 2	DAY 3	DAY 4	DAY 5	DAY 6
EXERCISE						
SETS						
REPS						
WEIGHTS						
REST TIME						

UPPER BODY						
EXERCISE						
SETS						
REPS						
WEIGHTS						
REST TIME						

LOWER BODY						
EXERCISE						
SETS						
REPS						
WEIGHTS						
REST TIME						

WARM UP	DAY 1	DAY 2	DAY 3	DAY 4	DAY 5	DAY 6
ACTIVITY						
SETS						
REPS						
TIME						
DIST						
INTENSITY						

COOL DOWN						
ACTIVITY						
SETS						
REPS						
TIME						
DIST						
INTENSITY						

GOALS: _____

_____

_____

_____

_____

_____

_____

_____

CORE BODY	DAY 1	DAY 2	DAY 3	DAY 4	DAY 5	DAY 6
EXERCISE						
SETS						
REPS						
WEIGHTS						
REST TIME						

UPPER BODY						
EXERCISE						
SETS						
REPS						
WEIGHTS						
REST TIME						

LOWER BODY						
EXERCISE						
SETS						
REPS						
WEIGHTS						
REST TIME						

WARM UP	DAY 1	DAY 2	DAY 3	DAY 4	DAY 5	DAY 6
ACTIVITY						
SETS						
REPS						
TIME						
DIST						
INTENSITY						
COOL DOWN						
ACTIVITY						
SETS						
REPS						
TIME						
DIST						
INTENSITY						

GOALS: _____

_____

_____

_____

_____

_____

_____

_____

CORE BODY	DAY 1	DAY 2	DAY 3	DAY 4	DAY 5	DAY 6
EXERCISE						
SETS						
REPS						
WEIGHTS						
REST TIME						

UPPER BODY						
EXERCISE						
SETS						
REPS						
WEIGHTS						
REST TIME						

LOWER BODY						
EXERCISE						
SETS						
REPS						
WEIGHTS						
REST TIME						

WARM UP	DAY 1	DAY 2	DAY 3	DAY 4	DAY 5	DAY 6
ACTIVITY						
SETS						
REPS						
TIME						
DIST						
INTENSITY						
COOL DOWN						
ACTIVITY						
SETS						
REPS						
TIME						
DIST						
INTENSITY						

GOALS: _____

_____

_____

_____

_____

_____

_____

_____

CORE BODY	DAY 1	DAY 2	DAY 3	DAY 4	DAY 5	DAY 6
EXERCISE						
SETS						
REPS						
WEIGHTS						
REST TIME						
UPPER BODY						
EXERCISE						
SETS						
REPS						
WEIGHTS						
REST TIME						
LOWER BODY						
EXERCISE						
SETS						
REPS						
WEIGHTS						
REST TIME						

WARM UP	DAY 1	DAY 2	DAY 3	DAY 4	DAY 5	DAY 6
ACTIVITY						
SETS						
REPS						
TIME						
DIST						
INTENSITY						

COOL DOWN						
ACTIVITY						
SETS						
REPS						
TIME						
DIST						
INTENSITY						

GOALS: _____

_____

_____

_____

_____

_____

_____

_____

CORE BODY	DAY 1	DAY 2	DAY 3	DAY 4	DAY 5	DAY 6
EXERCISE						
SETS						
REPS						
WEIGHTS						
REST TIME						

UPPER BODY						
EXERCISE						
SETS						
REPS						
WEIGHTS						
REST TIME						

LOWER BODY						
EXERCISE						
SETS						
REPS						
WEIGHTS						
REST TIME						

WARM UP	DAY 1	DAY 2	DAY 3	DAY 4	DAY 5	DAY 6
ACTIVITY						
SETS						
REPS						
TIME						
DIST						
INTENSITY						

COOL DOWN						
ACTIVITY						
SETS						
REPS						
TIME						
DIST						
INTENSITY						

GOALS: _____

_____

_____

_____

_____

_____

_____

_____

CORE BODY	DAY 1	DAY 2	DAY 3	DAY 4	DAY 5	DAY 6
EXERCISE						
SETS						
REPS						
WEIGHTS						
REST TIME						

UPPER BODY						
EXERCISE						
SETS						
REPS						
WEIGHTS						
REST TIME						

LOWER BODY						
EXERCISE						
SETS						
REPS						
WEIGHTS						
REST TIME						

WARM UP	DAY 1	DAY 2	DAY 3	DAY 4	DAY 5	DAY 6
ACTIVITY						
SETS						
REPS						
TIME						
DIST						
INTENSITY						
COOL DOWN						
ACTIVITY						
SETS						
REPS						
TIME						
DIST						
INTENSITY						

GOALS: _____

_____

_____

_____

_____

_____

_____

_____

CORE BODY	DAY 1	DAY 2	DAY 3	DAY 4	DAY 5	DAY 6
EXERCISE						
SETS						
REPS						
WEIGHTS						
REST TIME						

UPPER BODY						
EXERCISE						
SETS						
REPS						
WEIGHTS						
REST TIME						

LOWER BODY						
EXERCISE						
SETS						
REPS						
WEIGHTS						
REST TIME						

WARM UP	DAY 1	DAY 2	DAY 3	DAY 4	DAY 5	DAY 6
ACTIVITY						
SETS						
REPS						
TIME						
DIST						
INTENSITY						
COOL DOWN						
ACTIVITY						
SETS						
REPS						
TIME						
DIST						
INTENSITY						

GOALS: _____

_____

_____

_____

_____

_____

_____

_____

CORE BODY	DAY 1	DAY 2	DAY 3	DAY 4	DAY 5	DAY 6
EXERCISE						
SETS						
REPS						
WEIGHTS						
REST TIME						

UPPER BODY						
EXERCISE						
SETS						
REPS						
WEIGHTS						
REST TIME						

LOWER BODY						
EXERCISE						
SETS						
REPS						
WEIGHTS						
REST TIME						

WARM UP	DAY 1	DAY 2	DAY 3	DAY 4	DAY 5	DAY 6
ACTIVITY						
SETS						
REPS						
TIME						
DIST						
INTENSITY						

COOL DOWN						
ACTIVITY						
SETS						
REPS						
TIME						
DIST						
INTENSITY						

GOALS: _____

_____

_____

_____

_____

_____

_____

_____

CORE BODY	DAY 1	DAY 2	DAY 3	DAY 4	DAY 5	DAY 6
EXERCISE						
SETS						
REPS						
WEIGHTS						
REST TIME						
UPPER BODY						
EXERCISE						
SETS						
REPS						
WEIGHTS						
REST TIME						
LOWER BODY						
EXERCISE						
SETS						
REPS						
WEIGHTS						
REST TIME						

WARM UP	DAY 1	DAY 2	DAY 3	DAY 4	DAY 5	DAY 6
ACTIVITY						
SETS						
REPS						
TIME						
DIST						
INTENSITY						

COOL DOWN						
ACTIVITY						
SETS						
REPS						
TIME						
DIST						
INTENSITY						

GOALS: _____

_____

_____

_____

_____

_____

_____

_____

CORE BODY	DAY 1	DAY 2	DAY 3	DAY 4	DAY 5	DAY 6
EXERCISE						
SETS						
REPS						
WEIGHTS						
REST TIME						

UPPER BODY						
EXERCISE						
SETS						
REPS						
WEIGHTS						
REST TIME						

LOWER BODY						
EXERCISE						
SETS						
REPS						
WEIGHTS						
REST TIME						

WARM UP	DAY 1	DAY 2	DAY 3	DAY 4	DAY 5	DAY 6
ACTIVITY						
SETS						
REPS						
TIME						
DIST						
INTENSITY						

COOL DOWN						
ACTIVITY						
SETS						
REPS						
TIME						
DIST						
INTENSITY						

GOALS: _____

_____

_____

_____

_____

_____

_____

_____

CORE BODY	DAY 1	DAY 2	DAY 3	DAY 4	DAY 5	DAY 6
EXERCISE						
SETS						
REPS						
WEIGHTS						
REST TIME						

UPPER BODY						
EXERCISE						
SETS						
REPS						
WEIGHTS						
REST TIME						

LOWER BODY						
EXERCISE						
SETS						
REPS						
WEIGHTS						
REST TIME						

WARM UP	DAY 1	DAY 2	DAY 3	DAY 4	DAY 5	DAY 6
ACTIVITY						
SETS						
REPS						
TIME						
DIST						
INTENSITY						

COOL DOWN						
ACTIVITY						
SETS						
REPS						
TIME						
DIST						
INTENSITY						

GOALS: _____

_____

_____

_____

_____

_____

_____

_____

CORE BODY	DAY 1	DAY 2	DAY 3	DAY 4	DAY 5	DAY 6
EXERCISE						
SETS						
REPS						
WEIGHTS						
REST TIME						

UPPER BODY						
EXERCISE						
SETS						
REPS						
WEIGHTS						
REST TIME						

LOWER BODY						
EXERCISE						
SETS						
REPS						
WEIGHTS						
REST TIME						

WARM UP	DAY 1	DAY 2	DAY 3	DAY 4	DAY 5	DAY 6
ACTIVITY						
SETS						
REPS						
TIME						
DIST						
INTENSITY						

COOL DOWN						
ACTIVITY						
SETS						
REPS						
TIME						
DIST						
INTENSITY						

GOALS: _____

_____

_____

_____

_____

_____

_____

_____

CORE BODY	DAY 1	DAY 2	DAY 3	DAY 4	DAY 5	DAY 6
EXERCISE						
SETS						
REPS						
WEIGHTS						
REST TIME						

UPPER BODY						
EXERCISE						
SETS						
REPS						
WEIGHTS						
REST TIME						

LOWER BODY						
EXERCISE						
SETS						
REPS						
WEIGHTS						
REST TIME						

WARM UP	DAY 1	DAY 2	DAY 3	DAY 4	DAY 5	DAY 6
ACTIVITY						
SETS						
REPS						
TIME						
DIST						
INTENSITY						
COOL DOWN						
ACTIVITY						
SETS						
REPS						
TIME						
DIST						
INTENSITY						

GOALS: _____

_____

_____

_____

_____

_____

_____

_____

_____

CORE BODY	DAY 1	DAY 2	DAY 3	DAY 4	DAY 5	DAY 6
EXERCISE						
SETS						
REPS						
WEIGHTS						
REST TIME						

UPPER BODY						
EXERCISE						
SETS						
REPS						
WEIGHTS						
REST TIME						

LOWER BODY						
EXERCISE						
SETS						
REPS						
WEIGHTS						
REST TIME						

WARM UP	DAY 1	DAY 2	DAY 3	DAY 4	DAY 5	DAY 6
ACTIVITY						
SETS						
REPS						
TIME						
DIST						
INTENSITY						

COOL DOWN						
ACTIVITY						
SETS						
REPS						
TIME						
DIST						
INTENSITY						

GOALS: _____

_____

_____

_____

_____

_____

_____

_____

CORE BODY	DAY 1	DAY 2	DAY 3	DAY 4	DAY 5	DAY 6
EXERCISE						
SETS						
REPS						
WEIGHTS						
REST TIME						

UPPER BODY						
EXERCISE						
SETS						
REPS						
WEIGHTS						
REST TIME						

LOWER BODY						
EXERCISE						
SETS						
REPS						
WEIGHTS						
REST TIME						

WARM UP	DAY 1	DAY 2	DAY 3	DAY 4	DAY 5	DAY 6
ACTIVITY						
SETS						
REPS						
TIME						
DIST						
INTENSITY						
COOL DOWN						
ACTIVITY						
SETS						
REPS						
TIME						
DIST						
INTENSITY						

GOALS: _____

_____

_____

_____

_____

_____

_____

_____

_____

CORE BODY	DAY 1	DAY 2	DAY 3	DAY 4	DAY 5	DAY 6
EXERCISE						
SETS						
REPS						
WEIGHTS						
REST TIME						

UPPER BODY						
EXERCISE						
SETS						
REPS						
WEIGHTS						
REST TIME						

LOWER BODY						
EXERCISE						
SETS						
REPS						
WEIGHTS						
REST TIME						

WARM UP	DAY 1	DAY 2	DAY 3	DAY 4	DAY 5	DAY 6
ACTIVITY						
SETS						
REPS						
TIME						
DIST						
INTENSITY						

COOL DOWN						
ACTIVITY						
SETS						
REPS						
TIME						
DIST						
INTENSITY						

GOALS: _____

_____

_____

_____

_____

_____

_____

_____

CORE BODY	DAY 1	DAY 2	DAY 3	DAY 4	DAY 5	DAY 6
EXERCISE						
SETS						
REPS						
WEIGHTS						
REST TIME						
UPPER BODY						
EXERCISE						
SETS						
REPS						
WEIGHTS						
REST TIME						
LOWER BODY						
EXERCISE						
SETS						
REPS						
WEIGHTS						
REST TIME						

WARM UP	DAY 1	DAY 2	DAY 3	DAY 4	DAY 5	DAY 6
ACTIVITY						
SETS						
REPS						
TIME						
DIST						
INTENSITY						
COOL DOWN						
ACTIVITY						
SETS						
REPS						
TIME						
DIST						
INTENSITY						

GOALS: _____

_____

_____

_____

_____

_____

_____

_____

CORE BODY	DAY 1	DAY 2	DAY 3	DAY 4	DAY 5	DAY 6
EXERCISE						
SETS						
REPS						
WEIGHTS						
REST TIME						

UPPER BODY						
EXERCISE						
SETS						
REPS						
WEIGHTS						
REST TIME						

LOWER BODY						
EXERCISE						
SETS						
REPS						
WEIGHTS						
REST TIME						

WARM UP	DAY 1	DAY 2	DAY 3	DAY 4	DAY 5	DAY 6
ACTIVITY						
SETS						
REPS						
TIME						
DIST						
INTENSITY						

COOL DOWN						
ACTIVITY						
SETS						
REPS						
TIME						
DIST						
INTENSITY						

GOALS: _____

_____

_____

_____

_____

_____

_____

_____

CORE BODY	DAY 1	DAY 2	DAY 3	DAY 4	DAY 5	DAY 6
EXERCISE						
SETS						
REPS						
WEIGHTS						
REST TIME						

UPPER BODY						
EXERCISE						
SETS						
REPS						
WEIGHTS						
REST TIME						

LOWER BODY						
EXERCISE						
SETS						
REPS						
WEIGHTS						
REST TIME						

WARM UP	DAY 1	DAY 2	DAY 3	DAY 4	DAY 5	DAY 6
ACTIVITY						
SETS						
REPS						
TIME						
DIST						
INTENSITY						

COOL DOWN						
ACTIVITY						
SETS						
REPS						
TIME						
DIST						
INTENSITY						

GOALS: _____

_____

_____

_____

_____

_____

_____

_____

CORE BODY	DAY 1	DAY 2	DAY 3	DAY 4	DAY 5	DAY 6
EXERCISE						
SETS						
REPS						
WEIGHTS						
REST TIME						

UPPER BODY						
EXERCISE						
SETS						
REPS						
WEIGHTS						
REST TIME						

LOWER BODY						
EXERCISE						
SETS						
REPS						
WEIGHTS						
REST TIME						

WARM UP	DAY 1	DAY 2	DAY 3	DAY 4	DAY 5	DAY 6
ACTIVITY						
SETS						
REPS						
TIME						
DIST						
INTENSITY						

COOL DOWN						
ACTIVITY						
SETS						
REPS						
TIME						
DIST						
INTENSITY						

GOALS: _____

_____

_____

_____

_____

_____

_____

CORE BODY	DAY 1	DAY 2	DAY 3	DAY 4	DAY 5	DAY 6
EXERCISE						
SETS						
REPS						
WEIGHTS						
REST TIME						

UPPER BODY						
EXERCISE						
SETS						
REPS						
WEIGHTS						
REST TIME						

LOWER BODY						
EXERCISE						
SETS						
REPS						
WEIGHTS						
REST TIME						

WARM UP	DAY 1	DAY 2	DAY 3	DAY 4	DAY 5	DAY 6
ACTIVITY						
SETS						
REPS						
TIME						
DIST						
INTENSITY						
COOL DOWN						
ACTIVITY						
SETS						
REPS						
TIME						
DIST						
INTENSITY						

GOALS: _____

_____

_____

_____

_____

_____

_____

_____

CORE BODY	DAY 1	DAY 2	DAY 3	DAY 4	DAY 5	DAY 6
EXERCISE						
SETS						
REPS						
WEIGHTS						
REST TIME						

UPPER BODY						
EXERCICE						
SETS						
REPS						
WEIGHTS						
REST TIME						

LOWER BODY						
EXERCISE						
SETS						
REPS						
WEIGHTS						
REST TIME						

WARM UP	DAY 1	DAY 2	DAY 3	DAY 4	DAY 5	DAY 6
ACTIVITY						
SETS						
REPS						
TIME						
DIST						
INTENSITY						

COOL DOWN						
ACTIVITY						
SETS						
REPS						
TIME						
DIST						
INTENSITY						

GOALS: _____

_____

_____

_____

_____

_____

_____

_____

CORE BODY	DAY 1	DAY 2	DAY 3	DAY 4	DAY 5	DAY 6
EXERCISE						
SETS						
REPS						
WEIGHTS						
REST TIME						

UPPER BODY						
EXERCISE						
SETS						
REPS						
WEIGHTS						
REST TIME						

LOWER BODY						
EXERCISE						
SETS						
REPS						
WEIGHTS						
REST TIME						

WARM UP	DAY 1	DAY 2	DAY 3	DAY 4	DAY 5	DAY 6
ACTIVITY						
SETS						
REPS						
TIME						
DIST						
INTENSITY						

COOL DOWN						
ACTIVITY						
SETS						
REPS						
TIME						
DIST						
INTENSITY						

GOALS: _____

_____

_____

_____

_____

_____

_____

_____

CORE BODY	DAY 1	DAY 2	DAY 3	DAY 4	DAY 5	DAY 6
EXERCISE						
SETS						
REPS						
WEIGHTS						
REST TIME						

UPPER BODY						
EXERCISE						
SETS						
REPS						
WEIGHTS						
REST TIME						

LOWER BODY						
EXERCISE						
SETS						
REPS						
WEIGHTS						
REST TIME						

WARM UP	DAY 1	DAY 2	DAY 3	DAY 4	DAY 5	DAY 6
ACTIVITY						
SETS						
REPS						
TIME						
DIST						
INTENSITY						

COOL DOWN						
ACTIVITY						
SETS						
REPS						
TIME						
DIST						
INTENSITY						

GOALS: _____

_____

_____

_____

_____

_____

_____

_____

CORE BODY	DAY 1	DAY 2	DAY 3	DAY 4	DAY 5	DAY 6
EXERCISE						
SETS						
REPS						
WEIGHTS						
REST TIME						

UPPER BODY						
EXERCISE						
SETS						
REPS						
WEIGHTS						
REST TIME						

LOWER BODY						
EXERCISE						
SETS						
REPS						
WEIGHTS						
REST TIME						

WARM UP	DAY 1	DAY 2	DAY 3	DAY 4	DAY 5	DAY 6
ACTIVITY						
SETS						
REPS						
TIME						
DIST						
INTENSITY						
COOL DOWN						
ACTIVITY						
SETS						
REPS						
TIME						
DIST						
INTENSITY						

GOALS: _____

_____

_____

_____

_____

_____

_____

_____

CORE BODY	DAY 1	DAY 2	DAY 3	DAY 4	DAY 5	DAY 6
EXERCISE						
SETS						
REPS						
WEIGHTS						
REST TIME						

UPPER BODY						
EXERCISE						
SETS						
REPS						
WEIGHTS						
REST TIME						

LOWER BODY						
EXERCISE						
SETS						
REPS						
WEIGHTS						
REST TIME						

WARM UP	DAY 1	DAY 2	DAY 3	DAY 4	DAY 5	DAY 6
ACTIVITY						
SETS						
REPS						
TIME						
DIST						
INTENSITY						

COOL DOWN						
ACTIVITY						
SETS						
REPS						
TIME						
DIST						
INTENSITY						

GOALS: _____

_____

_____

_____

_____

_____

_____

_____

CORE BODY	DAY 1	DAY 2	DAY 3	DAY 4	DAY 5	DAY 6
EXERCISE						
SETS						
REPS						
WEIGHTS						
REST TIME						

UPPER BODY						
EXERCISE						
SETS						
REPS						
WEIGHTS						
REST TIME						

LOWER BODY						
EXERCISE						
SETS						
REPS						
WEIGHTS						
REST TIME						

WARM UP	DAY 1	DAY 2	DAY 3	DAY 4	DAY 5	DAY 6
ACTIVITY						
SETS						
REPS						
TIME						
DIST						
INTENSITY						
COOL DOWN						
ACTIVITY						
SETS						
REPS						
TIME						
DIST						
INTENSITY						

GOALS: _____

_____

_____

_____

_____

_____

_____

_____

CORE BODY	DAY 1	DAY 2	DAY 3	DAY 4	DAY 5	DAY 6
EXERCISE						
SETS						
REPS						
WEIGHTS						
REST TIME						

UPPER BODY						
EXERCISE						
SETS						
REPS						
WEIGHTS						
REST TIME						

LOWER BODY						
EXERCISE						
SETS						
REPS						
WEIGHTS						
REST TIME						

WARM UP	DAY 1	DAY 2	DAY 3	DAY 4	DAY 5	DAY 6
ACTIVITY						
SETS						
REPS						
TIME						
DIST						
INTENSITY						

COOL DOWN						
ACTIVITY						
SETS						
REPS						
TIME						
DIST						
INTENSITY						

GOALS: _____

_____

_____

_____

_____

_____

_____

CORE BODY	DAY 1	DAY 2	DAY 3	DAY 4	DAY 5	DAY 6
EXERCISE						
SETS						
REPS						
WEIGHTS						
REST TIME						
UPPER BODY						
EXERCISE						
SETS						
REPS						
WEIGHTS						
REST TIME						
LOWER BODY						
EXERCISE						
SETS						
REPS						
WEIGHTS						
REST TIME						

WARM UP	DAY 1	DAY 2	DAY 3	DAY 4	DAY 5	DAY 6
ACTIVITY						
SETS						
REPS						
TIME						
DIST						
INTENSITY						
COOL DOWN						
ACTIVITY						
SETS						
REPS						
TIME						
DIST						
INTENSITY						

GOALS: _____

_____

_____

_____

_____

_____

_____

_____

CORE BODY	DAY 1	DAY 2	DAY 3	DAY 4	DAY 5	DAY 6
EXERCISE						
SETS						
REPS						
WEIGHTS						
REST TIME						

UPPER BODY						
EXERCISE						
SETS						
REPS						
WEIGHTS						
REST TIME						

LOWER BODY						
EXERCISE						
SETS						
REPS						
WEIGHTS						
REST TIME						

WARM UP	DAY 1	DAY 2	DAY 3	DAY 4	DAY 5	DAY 6
ACTIVITY						
SETS						
REPS						
TIME						
DIST						
INTENSITY						

COOL DOWN						
ACTIVITY						
SETS						
REPS						
TIME						
DIST						
INTENSITY						

GOALS: _____

_____

_____

_____

_____

_____

_____

_____

CORE BODY	DAY 1	DAY 2	DAY 3	DAY 4	DAY 5	DAY 6
EXERCISE						
SETS						
REPS						
WEIGHTS						
REST TIME						

UPPER BODY						
EXERCISE						
SETS						
REPS						
WEIGHTS						
REST TIME						

LOWER BODY						
EXERCISE						
SETS						
REPS						
WEIGHTS						
REST TIME						

WARM UP	DAY 1	DAY 2	DAY 3	DAY 4	DAY 5	DAY 6
ACTIVITY						
SETS						
REPS						
TIME						
DIST						
INTENSITY						
COOL DOWN						
ACTIVITY						
SETS						
REPS						
TIME						
DIST						
INTENSITY						

GOALS: _____

_____

_____

_____

_____

_____

_____

_____

CORE BODY	DAY 1	DAY 2	DAY 3	DAY 4	DAY 5	DAY 6
EXERCISE						
SETS						
REPS						
WEIGHTS						
REST TIME						

UPPER BODY						
EXERCISE						
SETS						
REPS						
WEIGHTS						
REST TIME						

LOWER BODY						
EXERCISE						
SETS						
REPS						
WEIGHTS						
REST TIME						

WARM UP	DAY 1	DAY 2	DAY 3	DAY 4	DAY 5	DAY 6
ACTIVITY						
SETS						
REPS						
TIME						
DIST						
INTENSITY						
COOL DOWN						
ACTIVITY						
SETS						
REPS						
TIME						
DIST						
INTENSITY						

GOALS: _____

_____

_____

_____

_____

_____

_____

_____

CORE BODY	DAY 1	DAY 2	DAY 3	DAY 4	DAY 5	DAY 6
EXERCISE						
SETS						
REPS						
WEIGHTS						
REST TIME						

UPPER BODY						
EXERCISE						
SETS						
REPS						
WEIGHTS						
REST TIME						

LOWER BODY						
EXERCISE						
SETS						
REPS						
WEIGHTS						
REST TIME						

WARM UP	DAY 1	DAY 2	DAY 3	DAY 4	DAY 5	DAY 6
ACTIVITY						
SETS						
REPS						
TIME						
DIST						
INTENSITY						
COOL DOWN						
ACTIVITY						
SETS						
REPS						
TIME						
DIST						
INTENSITY						

GOALS: _____

_____

_____

_____

_____

_____

_____

_____

CORE BODY	DAY 1	DAY 2	DAY 3	DAY 4	DAY 5	DAY 6
EXERCISE						
SETS						
REPS						
WEIGHTS						
REST TIME						

UPPER BODY						
EXERCISE						
SETS						
REPS						
WEIGHTS						
REST TIME						

LOWER BODY						
EXERCISE						
SETS						
REPS						
WEIGHTS						
REST TIME						

WARM UP	DAY 1	DAY 2	DAY 3	DAY 4	DAY 5	DAY 6
ACTIVITY						
SETS						
REPS						
TIME						
DIST						
INTENSITY						
COOL DOWN						
ACTIVITY						
SETS						
REPS						
TIME						
DIST						
INTENSITY						

GOALS: _____

_____

_____

_____

_____

_____

_____

_____

_____

CORE BODY	DAY 1	DAY 2	DAY 3	DAY 4	DAY 5	DAY 6
EXERCISE						
SETS						
REPS						
WEIGHTS						
REST TIME						

UPPER BODY						
EXERCISE						
SETS						
REPS						
WEIGHTS						
REST TIME						

LOWER BODY						
EXERCISE						
SETS						
REPS						
WEIGHTS						
REST TIME						

WARM UP	DAY 1	DAY 2	DAY 3	DAY 4	DAY 5	DAY 6
ACTIVITY						
SETS						
REPS						
TIME						
DIST						
INTENSITY						

COOL DOWN						
ACTIVITY						
SETS						
REPS						
TIME						
DIST						
INTENSITY						

GOALS: _____

_____

_____

_____

_____

_____

_____

_____

CORE BODY	DAY 1	DAY 2	DAY 3	DAY 4	DAY 5	DAY 6
EXERCISE						
SETS						
REPS						
WEIGHTS						
REST TIME						

UPPER BODY						
EXERCISE						
SETS						
REPS						
WEIGHTS						
REST TIME						

LOWER BODY						
EXERCISE						
SETS						
REPS						
WEIGHTS						
REST TIME						

WARM UP	DAY 1	DAY 2	DAY 3	DAY 4	DAY 5	DAY 6
ACTIVITY						
SETS						
REPS						
TIME						
DIST						
INTENSITY						
COOL DOWN						
ACTIVITY						
SETS						
REPS						
TIME						
DIST						
INTENSITY						

GOALS: _____

_____

_____

_____

_____

_____

_____

_____

CORE BODY	DAY 1	DAY 2	DAY 3	DAY 4	DAY 5	DAY 6
EXERCISE						
SETS						
REPS						
WEIGHTS						
REST TIME						

UPPER BODY						
EXERCISE						
SETS						
REPS						
WEIGHTS						
REST TIME						

LOWER BODY						
EXERCISE						
SETS						
REPS						
WEIGHTS						
REST TIME						

WARM UP	DAY 1	DAY 2	DAY 3	DAY 4	DAY 5	DAY 6
ACTIVITY						
SETS						
REPS						
TIME						
DIST						
INTENSITY						

COOL DOWN						
ACTIVITY						
SETS						
REPS						
TIME						
DIST						
INTENSITY						

GOALS: _____

_____

_____

_____

_____

_____

_____

_____

CORE BODY	DAY 1	DAY 2	DAY 3	DAY 4	DAY 5	DAY 6
EXERCISE						
SETS						
REPS						
WEIGHTS						
REST TIME						

UPPER BODY						
EXERCISE						
SETS						
REPS						
WEIGHTS						
REST TIME						

LOWER BODY						
EXERCISE						
SETS						
REPS						
WEIGHTS						
REST TIME						

WARM UP	DAY 1	DAY 2	DAY 3	DAY 4	DAY 5	DAY 6
ACTIVITY						
SETS						
REPS						
TIME						
DIST						
INTENSITY						

COOL DOWN						
ACTIVITY						
SETS						
REPS						
TIME						
DIST						
INTENSITY						

GOALS: _____

_____

_____

_____

_____

_____

_____

_____

CORE BODY	DAY 1	DAY 2	DAY 3	DAY 4	DAY 5	DAY 6
EXERCISE						
SETS						
REPS						
WEIGHTS						
REST TIME						

UPPER BODY						
EXERCISE						
SETS						
REPS						
WEIGHTS						
REST TIME						

LOWER BODY						
EXERCISE						
SETS						
REPS						
WEIGHTS						
REST TIME						

WARM UP	DAY 1	DAY 2	DAY 3	DAY 4	DAY 5	DAY 6
ACTIVITY						
SETS						
REPS						
TIME						
DIST						
INTENSITY						
COOL DOWN						
ACTIVITY						
SETS						
REPS						
TIME						
DIST						
INTENSITY						

GOALS: _____

_____

_____

_____

_____

_____

_____

_____

CORE BODY	DAY 1	DAY 2	DAY 3	DAY 4	DAY 5	DAY 6
EXERCISE						
SETS						
REPS						
WEIGHTS						
REST TIME						
UPPER BODY						
EXERCISE						
SETS						
REPS						
WEIGHTS						
REST TIME						
LOWER BODY						
EXERCISE						
SETS						
REPS						
WEIGHTS						
REST TIME						

WARM UP	DAY 1	DAY 2	DAY 3	DAY 4	DAY 5	DAY 6
ACTIVITY						
SETS						
REPS						
TIME						
DIST						
INTENSITY						

COOL DOWN						
ACTIVITY						
SETS						
REPS						
TIME						
DIST						
INTENSITY						

GOALS: _____

_____

_____

_____

_____

_____

_____

_____

CORE BODY	DAY 1	DAY 2	DAY 3	DAY 4	DAY 5	DAY 6
EXERCISE						
SETS						
REPS						
WEIGHTS						
REST TIME						

UPPER BODY						
EXERCISE						
SETS						
REPS						
WEIGHTS						
REST TIME						

LOWER BODY						
EXERCISE						
SETS						
REPS						
WEIGHTS						
REST TIME						

WARM UP	DAY 1	DAY 2	DAY 3	DAY 4	DAY 5	DAY 6
ACTIVITY						
SETS						
REPS						
TIME						
DIST						
INTENSITY						

COOL DOWN						
ACTIVITY						
SETS						
REPS						
TIME						
DIST						
INTENSITY						

GOALS: _____

_____

_____

_____

_____

_____

_____

_____

CORE BODY	DAY 1	DAY 2	DAY 3	DAY 4	DAY 5	DAY 6
EXERCISE						
SETS						
REPS						
WEIGHTS						
REST TIME						

UPPER BODY						
EXERCISE						
SETS						
REPS						
WEIGHTS						
REST TIME						

LOWER BODY						
EXERCISE						
SETS						
REPS						
WEIGHTS						
REST TIME						

WARM UP	DAY 1	DAY 2	DAY 3	DAY 4	DAY 5	DAY 6
ACTIVITY						
SETS						
REPS						
TIME						
DIST						
INTENSITY						
COOL DOWN						
ACTIVITY						
SETS						
REPS						
TIME						
DIST						
INTENSITY						

GOALS: _____

_____

_____

_____

_____

_____

_____

_____

CORE BODY	DAY 1	DAY 2	DAY 3	DAY 4	DAY 5	DAY 6
EXERCISE						
SETS						
REPS						
WEIGHTS						
REST TIME						

UPPER BODY						
EXERCISE						
SETS						
REPS						
WEIGHTS						
REST TIME						

LOWER BODY						
EXERCISE						
SETS						
REPS						
WEIGHTS						
REST TIME						

WARM UP	DAY 1	DAY 2	DAY 3	DAY 4	DAY 5	DAY 6
ACTIVITY						
SETS						
REPS						
TIME						
DIST						
INTENSITY						
COOL DOWN						
ACTIVITY						
SETS						
REPS						
TIME						
DIST						
INTENSITY						

GOALS: _____

_____

_____

_____

_____

_____

_____

_____

CORE BODY	DAY 1	DAY 2	DAY 3	DAY 4	DAY 5	DAY 6
EXERCISE						
SETS						
REPS						
WEIGHTS						
REST TIME						
UPPER BODY						
EXERCISE						
SETS						
REPS						
WEIGHTS						
REST TIME						
LOWER BODY						
EXERCISE						
SETS						
REPS						
WEIGHTS						
REST TIME						

WARM UP	DAY 1	DAY 2	DAY 3	DAY 4	DAY 5	DAY 6
ACTIVITY						
SETS						
REPS						
TIME						
DIST						
INTENSITY						

COOL DOWN						
ACTIVITY						
SETS						
REPS						
TIME						
DIST						
INTENSITY						

GOALS: _____

_____

_____

_____

_____

_____

_____

_____

CORE BODY	DAY 1	DAY 2	DAY 3	DAY 4	DAY 5	DAY 6
EXERCISE						
SETS						
REPS						
WEIGHTS						
REST TIME						

UPPER BODY						
EXERCISE						
SETS						
REPS						
WEIGHTS						
REST TIME						

LOWER BODY						
EXERCISE						
SETS						
REPS						
WEIGHTS						
REST TIME						

WARM UP	DAY 1	DAY 2	DAY 3	DAY 4	DAY 5	DAY 6
ACTIVITY						
SETS						
REPS						
TIME						
DIST						
INTENSITY						
COOL DOWN						
ACTIVITY						
SETS						
REPS						
TIME						
DIST						
INTENSITY						

GOALS: _____

_____

_____

_____

_____

_____

_____

_____

CORE BODY	DAY 1	DAY 2	DAY 3	DAY 4	DAY 5	DAY 6
EXERCISE						
SETS						
REPS						
WEIGHTS						
REST TIME						

UPPER BODY						
EXERCISE						
SETS						
REPS						
WEIGHTS						
REST TIME						

LOWER BODY						
EXERCISE						
SETS						
REPS						
WEIGHTS						
REST TIME						

WARM UP	DAY 1	DAY 2	DAY 3	DAY 4	DAY 5	DAY 6
ACTIVITY						
SETS						
REPS						
TIME						
DIST						
INTENSITY						

COOL DOWN						
ACTIVITY						
SETS						
REPS						
TIME						
DIST						
INTENSITY						

GOALS: _____

_____

_____

_____

_____

_____

_____

_____

CORE BODY	DAY 1	DAY 2	DAY 3	DAY 4	DAY 5	DAY 6
EXERCISE						
SETS						
REPS						
WEIGHTS						
REST TIME						

UPPER BODY						
EXERCISE						
SETS						
REPS						
WEIGHTS						
REST TIME						

LOWER BODY						
EXERCISE						
SETS						
REPS						
WEIGHTS						
REST TIME						

WARM UP	DAY 1	DAY 2	DAY 3	DAY 4	DAY 5	DAY 6
ACTIVITY						
SETS						
REPS						
TIME						
DIST						
INTENSITY						
COOL DOWN						
ACTIVITY						
SETS						
REPS						
TIME						
DIST						
INTENSITY						

GOALS: _____

_____

_____

_____

_____

_____

_____

_____

www.ingramcontent.com/pod-product-compliance
Lightning Source LLC
Chambersburg PA
CBHW080738250626
47170CB00010B/2871